HANDS-ON
PIONEERS
ART ACTIVITIES FOR ALL AGES

To the generations of pioneer descendants who might continue making objects
like those their ancestors created and valued.

Mary Simpson illustrated the map and the activity pages.

Jim Tilly, Jennifer Moody, and Joni Sweetman, graphic designers,
and Sasha Sagan, artist and photographer,
of Art and International Productions in Anchorage, Alaska,
assisted in producing the book.

Deseret Book publishing staff who were essential in this book's publication were
Sheri Dew, Devan Jensen, Anne Sheffield, and Michelle Eckersley.

© 1995 Yvonne Young Merrill

First printing October 1995
Printed in China

Library of Congress Catalog Card Number 95-70453

ISBN 1-57345-085-5

HANDS-ON
PIONEERS

ART ACTIVITIES FOR ALL AGES

YVONNE YOUNG MERRILL
with
EMILY YOUNG MERRILL

DESERET BOOK COMPANY
SALT LAKE CITY, UTAH

CONTENTS

OUR PHILOSOPHY

As parents, teachers, or youth leaders, we may find it challenging to battle for a child's attention amid high-tech games, action heroes, and push-button entertainment. *Hands-on Pioneers* competes with passive activities by offering interactive projects that are engaging, educational, and rewarding.

As Erik Erikson wrote, "Play is serious business." We know that important development takes place while children are rolling clay, folding paper, kneading dough, printing designs, brushing paint, cutting, gluing, tying, and viewing the finished product with pride. An ancient Chinese proverb explains:

> I hear and I forget.
> I see and I remember.
> I do and I understand.

By combining hands-on exploration with real-life historical events, we give creative expression another dimension. *Hands-on Pioneers* brings to life the pioneers' quiet but deeply important part of the American story. Pioneers were among history's true action heroes; their real-life challenges and adventures easily rival the exploits of fantasy figures or cartoon characters.

Most children thrive on creative expression. This book emphasizes the *process* of creation and the *joy* of discovery. *Hands-on Pioneers* is designed to assist the leader who accepts a seagull that is colored orange and who doesn't mind if a sunbonnet is crooked or a gingerbread doll is nibbled. Regardless of the outcome, we hope these products will help children form a link to early pioneers and their culture.

Perhaps you teach restless children for one hour a week. Perhaps you know children eager for variety. Perhaps neighbor children venture into your yard to explore and you hear "I'm bored" or "What can I do?" *Hands-on Pioneers* can help children fill the hours by having fun while doing engaging activities.

HOW TO USE THIS BOOK

This book includes games, crafts, and historical background and stories. It is divided into 4 sections: 3 activity sections and the pattern pages.

The activity sections begin with double-page photographs of museum artifacts. On these photos, a seek-and-find game challenges children to search for specific items. The answer key in the back of the book identifies the items and explains their history based on information from museum records. Knowing the background of the artifacts enhances the pioneer story. To find out about the resource materials shown on this page, turn to page 82.

Patterns are included in the last section. We hope you will modify them to express your individuality. For personal use, you may photocopy the pattern pages so that you do not have to damage the book. You will then be able to save the copied pages and reuse them.

HINTS FOR PARENTS OR TEACHERS
- Entertain children on a rainy day with the seek-and-find games or the activities.
- Base family night activities on one of the stories or crafts.
- Make one of the crafts while teaching about the pioneers.
- Use this book as a resource for developing a history unit.
- Combine a hands-on activity with a visit to a museum or historical park.
- Create and give presents based on the activity ideas.
- Make the ox or seagull mask and create a simple costume.
- Involve young people at a family reunion with fun activities that teach about the past.

TOOLS

We have made every effort to use accessible, inexpensive, safe tools and materials for the projects in this book. Our decorating tools are common to most households, schools, and community programs. They include:

- wax crayons
- washable and sometimes permanent markers
- oil pastels
- washable acrylic paint
- tempera paint
- a watercolor brush with a small tip
- a utility knife (adult supervision is recommended)
- a hot-glue or craft gun (handy, but this tool gets dangerously hot and should be used only with adult supervision)

MATERIALS

We have tried to produce nearly all activities with paper. We rely on:

- poster board, available in most supermarkets
- file folders, which you may be discarding
- construction paper, available in packets of many colors
- butcher paper, which comes on large rolls and is now available in art and school supply stores, copy stores, and all schools
- plain newsprint, inexpensive and available from most printing companies
- tissue paper, crepe paper, and paper plates

We encourage you to use everyday, throwaway items. This saves you money and recycles potentially useful items that could stimulate creativity. Such items include fabric scraps, old socks, sticks and dowel scraps, buttons, fishing line, well-washed plain cotton handkerchiefs, and T-shirts.

Use your imagination when choosing materials. If you don't have a paint tray, use a paper plate, pie tin, or foil-covered pan (if you cover any pan with foil, paint cleanup is easier).

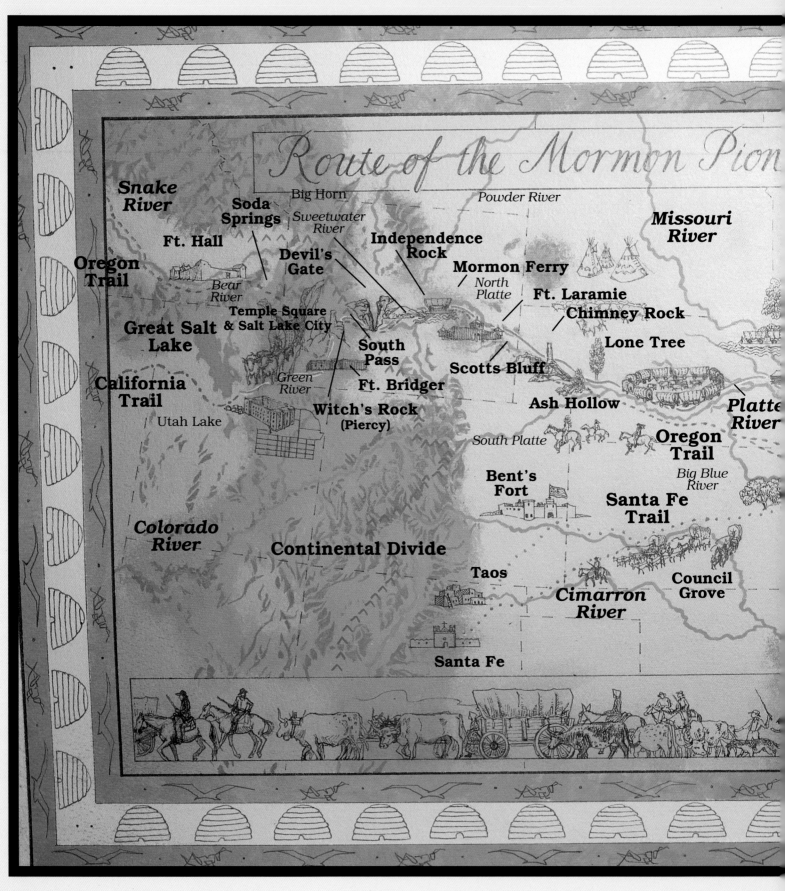

Route of the Mormon Pion[eers]

Snake River

Soda Springs

Big Horn

Powder River

Missouri River

Ft. Hall

Sweetwater River

Independence Rock

Oregon Trail

Devil's Gate

Bear River

Mormon Ferry

Ft. Laramie

North Platte

Chimney Rock

Temple Square & Salt Lake City

Great Salt Lake

South Pass

Lone Tree

California Trail

Green River

Ft. Bridger

Scotts Bluff

Utah Lake

Witch's Rock (Piercy)

Ash Hollow

Platte River

South Platte

Oregon Trail

Big Blue River

Bent's Fort

Santa Fe Trail

Colorado River

Continental Divide

Taos

Cimarron River

Council Grove

Santa Fe

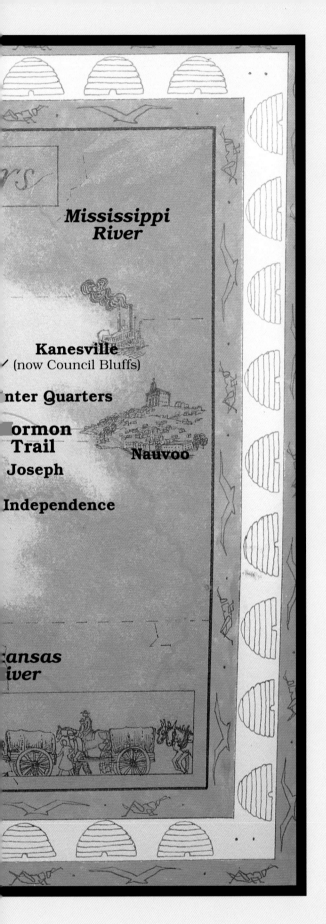

Mississippi
River

Kanesville
(now Council Bluffs)

nter Quarters

ormon
Trail

Joseph   Nauvoo

Independence

ansas
iver

THE MORMON PIONEER TRAIL

The Mormon migration has been called the most organized, systematic, and successful exodus in American history. Mormons—members of The Church of Jesus Christ of Latter-day Saints— pulled handcarts over the 1,400-mile journey from Nauvoo, Illinois, to the Great Salt Lake Valley. Surely to the trekkers from the lush midwestern and eastern United States this promised land was a disappointment. The desert plain was also inhospitable to the Ute Indians who came into the valley only when they were searching for crickets to eat.

The industrious Saints hitched up plows within two hours of their arrival. Planting had begun! A creek was dammed to bring water to the hardened ground. By the end of the first day, garden plots were parceled out and the first camp was made, consisting of 143 men, 3 women, and 2 children. The first potato crop was planted the next day. Within a month, a fort and 29 adobe brick houses were built. As later pioneer parties trickled into the valley, they built dams, tanneries, mills, log homes and selected the site for the Salt Lake Temple.

The early settlers built their communities with simple resources but great capacity. They possessed skills and craftsmanship honed in eastern towns and European cities. Available materials were used with ingenuity, hard work, and patience. Their homes were soon decorated. Worn household items were replaced with newly crafted treasures.

Pioneer stories are remarkable and inspiring. As a group, the pioneers harnessed practicality, discipline, and deep faith to quickly build an empire. Individually they experienced sorrow, struggles, great joy, and satisfaction in their work. Their remaining personal items demonstrate their creativity. Those items, many of them more than 150 years old, are gentle reminders of the pioneers' enterprising spirit.

Pioneer Children's Treasures

Pioneer children's clothing and toys were usually made of discarded parts. Clothing was often handed down or sewn large and tucked and hemmed temporarily as the wearer grew. Toys were contrived of odds and ends— a doll's dress was made from a tattered pinafore; a hobbyhorse head was sewn from holey socks. Few toys remain today of a pioneer child's pastimes. Dolls, tops, and games were made to be used and were passed around until they wore out. Their worth is not only in their rarity but also in their history.

CAN YOU FIND a game board, a fancy leather shoe, a dress made of many

patches, a doll's chair, a handmade ball, part of a school picture, a black slipper? *Answers on page 83.*

Tops

TOPS

Materials: poster board or a file folder, round lid or compass, ruler, scissors, pencil, colored markers, masking tape, nail or toothpick with pointed ends for spinning.

1. On the poster board or file folder, draw several circles with a compass, or trace around a lid. *Make small circles; tops over 3 inches in diameter don't spin well.* Mark the center using a ruler.

2. Cut out your tops.

3. With a pencil and a ruler divide each top into sections: halves, thirds, quarters, and so on.

4. Use markers to draw designs like the pioneer designs shown or use your own ideas. You may repeat the same design several times or alternate designs in sectioned parts.

5. Press the nail or toothpick through the center hole. Spin. If the spinner begins to slip, attach pieces of masking tape to keep it in place.

EASY SCIENCE PROJECT
Try a science project in mixing colors. If you color one top half red and half blue, what color will you see when you spin the top? Try it. If you guessed purple, you are right. Remember that yellow and blue make green, and red and yellow make orange.

During the long journey across the plains, pioneer children cherished their pocket toys. One boy carried a small wooden top. The boy's wagon train cared for a lost Indian child. The lonesome boy was fascinated with the top and a friendship developed. Weeks later, when the Indian child's family was found, the pioneer boy gave the Indian child his treasured wooden top.

A SIMPLE SUNBONNET

A SIMPLE SUNBONNET

Materials: paper plate, rectangular piece of cloth or crepe paper (must be large enough to cover the wearer's head), stapler, glue, ribbons for ties, scissors, markers or crayons, additional ribbon for streamers.

1. Put paper plate face up. To make the rim of the bonnet, cut a wedge from the paper plate and cut out the center of the plate as shown.

2. Decorate front part of rim.

3. Make small triangle-shaped cuts along inside edge of rim; bend tabs back.

4. To make the back drape of the bonnet, gather the long side of the rectangular cloth or paper and staple it to the tabs. If you are using paper, you may glue it to the tabs.

5. On sides of bonnet, bring cloth edges A and B together to make a tuck. Staple tuck to ends of rim to create a head shape in the sunbonnet.

6. Attach ribbons for ties.

Head coverings were not only decorative but necessary for the pioneers. Sunbonnets shielded the women's eyes from the sun, wind, and dust. The back drape protected the neck. They were made from inexpensive calico or denim.

Men wore hats made from skins or hides. Both men and women made straw hats from locally grown straw that was braided and then sewn into a hat.

Hop-Along Hobbyhorse

Hop-Along Hobbyhorse

Materials: a large, clean, knee-high sock, a 1-inch-thick dowel about 36 inches long, yarn for the mane, 4 buttons or 4 brown felt circles (2 for eyes and 2 for nostrils), felt for ears, embroidery floss for facial details such as mouth and eyelashes, glue, batting for sock head, needle with a large eye, rawhide laces or string for reins, thread (optional, used for sewing on buttons for eyes and nostrils).

1. Decide on the placement of the button or felt eyes and nose by putting your hand inside the sock. Glue or sew eyes and nostrils in place.

2. Make the mouth with a running in-and-out stitch along the sock toe seam.

3. Cut felt ears. Make a pleat in the ears by folding felt from point A to point B. Sew ears on each side of the head.

4. To make the mane, thread yarn into a large-eyed needle. Loop yarn and knot at base of each strand. Cut loops.

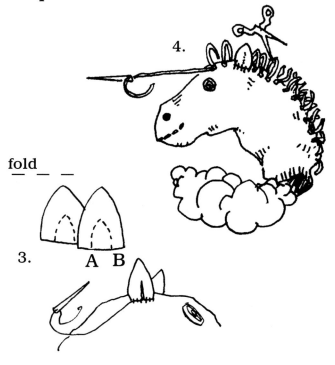

1.

2.

3.

fold _ _ _

A B

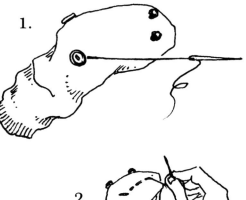

5. Stuff sock head with batting or old nylons. You will have to stuff tightly to avoid a limp and floppy horse.

6. Place the dowel end into the batting at least 8 to 10 inches. To keep batting enclosed, glue leg end of sock to dowel. Grasp the glued section firmly while it dries or wrap it with several rubber bands. Let glue dry overnight.

7. Add reins of string or rawhide shoelaces. Wrap reins several times around the sock base. Knot the ends securely.

Horses were not a luxury to early settlers; they were necessary for work and transportation. The Utah breeds were among the best in the country. Their lungs were strong from breathing thin, clean mountain air; the dry climate contributed to stronger hooves; and their muscles were powerful from long travels.

Imaginative children fashioned horses from everyday materials, often making heads and bodies from socks, carved wood, or bunched twigs.

GINGERBREAD DOLL PUPPETS

GINGERBREAD DOLL PUPPETS

Materials: ingredients for gingerbread cookies, ingredients for icing and icing tube with fine-point applicator (or buy ready-made icing in applicators, sold in the baking section of your grocery store), electric mixer, licorice strings, small candies (silver balls, red hots, and so on), garlic press, cookie sheet, patterns on page 65, ribbon or yarn for tying arms and legs, spatula, drinking straw or nail, large-eyed needle.

1. Make the gingerbread cookie dough. One recipe makes 8 10-inch to 12-inch dolls.

RECIPE FOR GINGERBREAD COOKIE DOUGH
Combine: 1 cup sugar
          1 cup shortening
          1 cup molasses
          1 egg

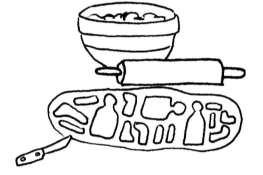

Sift: 5 1/2 cups flour
    1 teaspoon soda
    1 teaspoon salt
    3 teaspoons cinnamon
    2 teaspoons ginger
    2 teaspoons cloves
    1 teaspoon nutmeg

Combine first set of ingredients, then add sifted ingredients. You may need to add 1/2 to 1 cup of milk to moisten dough. Roll out dough 1/4 inch thick or thicker. The thicker the dough, the stronger the doll.

RECIPE FOR ICING
3 egg whites
4 1/2 cups (1 pound) powdered sugar
1 teaspoon vanilla
1/2 teaspoon cream of tartar

Combine ingredients and beat with electric mixer 7 to 9 minutes or until icing is stiff.

2. With scissors, cut out puppet patterns found on page 65.

3. On the rolled-out cookie dough, trace around the patterns with a knife. Cut out the body, legs, and arms. Carefully lift the dough shapes onto greased cookie sheets with a spatula.

4. Put holes in the arms and leg tops with the bottom of a drinking straw or a thick nail point. Make 8 holes—4 on the body and 1 on each arm and leg. If you are going to hang the doll for a decoration, you should also poke a hole 1/2 inch down from the top of the head.

5. Decorate the doll with licorice strings, silver balls, red hot candies, and so on. To create hair for the dolls, roll small coils of dough and lay them in curls, or force dough through a garlic press to create fine hair. *Icing is applied after the dough dolls are cooked and have cooled.*

6. Bake at 300 degrees Fahrenheit for 8 to 10 minutes. Cookies should be slightly brown on the bottom. Let cool before final assembly.

7. Connect the arms and legs to the body using yarn threaded through a large-eyed needle or by using your fingers to poke ribbon or yarn ends through the holes. Tie knots or strong bows.

8. Decorate doll using icing and an icing tube with a fine-point applicator.

Pioneers cooked with a few essential foods. Flour was the most important of all. Second was a sweetener. Pioneer women and girls would harvest sugar beets, mill them into pulp, and then boil and skim the mixture until ready for use.

Pioneers liked sweets. They made sorghum molasses, sweetened cakes, fruit preserves, and candy. Gingerbread dolls were a favorite holiday surprise. The spicy scent added to their appeal. These dolls can be used as puppets, holiday ornaments, or yummy cookies.

Pioneer Dolls

Dolls are a part of nearly every culture. The corn harvest meant a new corn husk doll for pioneer children. Pioneer children also made dolls from rocks, potatoes, eggshells, clothespins, nuts, corncobs, rags, wooden spoons, hollyhock blossoms, twigs, and gingerbread. Pioneer dolls had heads but frequently lacked bodies, arms, or legs. Doll hair was made from yarn, hide strips, corn silk, or human hair. Features were embroidered or painted on with berry juice, paint, or ink. Early pioneer dolls often had layers of faces indicating that worn-out features were replaced with new ones.

CAN YOU FIND the tallest doll, the dolls made of corn husks, the smallest and oldest rag doll with real human hair. Minerva (the fancy doll in a hat

with a green ribbon), two dolls made from twigs, a doll made from a
handkerchief? *Answers on page 82.*

CORN HUSK DOLLS

Materials: fresh, washed corn husks (corn husks were washed for new dolls after the harvest; you can either do this or buy tamale wrappers), scissors, string or yarn, scraps of cloth, glue.

1. Strip three clean, unbroken husks from the second layer of husks on the corn.

2. Lay the husks one over another. Roll a small ball of paper towel or tissue and place it in the center of the husks.

3. Fold corn husks evenly around the ball to make a head. Tie firmly at neck with string or yarn. Snip ends.

4. Make arms from a narrow piece of tightly rolled husk. Fold two ends so they overlap in the middle. This middle part will be held in place by the doll's body (see illustration).

5. Wrap waist of doll with string. Tie securely and snip ends.

6. Dress your doll with a bright kerchief and apron. Glue it in place. You may want to add some yarn or corn silk hair.

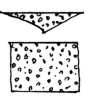

HANKIE DOLL

Materials: an iron, square piece of muslin or cotton cloth (any size square; ours is made from a 10-inch by 10-inch square), thread, needle, straight pins, scissors, cotton ball the size of an apricot, cotton swab, small calico print or any printed fabric scraps.

1. Wash and iron your piece of cloth. Lay out cloth; fold up a 1/2-inch hem and iron it.

2. Gather each corner and wrap thread around the gathers. You are making hands and feet that are each about 1/2 inch long.

3. Place a cotton ball in the center of the square and gather in the neck. Wrap thread around the neck. Tie firmly. Snip the ends.

4. Push and pull the fabric until you can see 2 arms in front and 2 legs behind. Pin hem and sew it with a slip stitch.

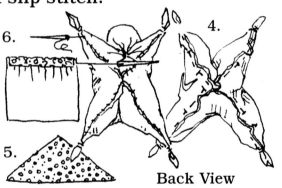

Back View

Front view

5. For a kerchief, cut a triangle 4 to 5 inches wide at the long triangle side.

6. For an apron, cut a 3-inch square. With needle and thread, gather the apron at the top and sew ends together at back.

7. Give doll cross-stitched eyes and pink cheeks (with blush on a cotton swab).

It is astonishing to learn of the crude materials pioneers lovingly cut and combined to create a doll for a child. One story tells of a rag doll made from clothing found on a shallow grave. But the doll had to be taken away and the girl placed under quarantine. The clothing had belonged to cholera victims traveling an early western trail.

TWIG DOLL

Materials: a twig with branches forked like arms and legs or a forked twig and a straight twig, a nut (we recommend a walnut, acorn, or hazelnut) for the head, scraps of cloth, a hot-glue gun or craft glue, paint or permanent markers for the face, yarn for hair, an electric drill with a small bit (optional but useful if you are working with a large group).

1. Have a good time finding your twig. If it is too tough to break off, ask an adult to help you cut it.

2. Cut out printed cloth for clothes using the simple patterns below.

3. If your stick lacks arms or legs, attach them with yarn as shown.

4. Cut a neck opening in shirt fabric. Slip shirt over stick "neck."

5. Attach head with a hot-glue gun. If you have an electric drill with a small bit, an adult can drill a hole in the bottom of the nut and push it onto the stick "neck." You may want to add the additional strength of hot glue or craft glue.

6. Paint or draw the face with permanent markers.

7. Gather the shirt at the waist and tie it in place. Glue skirt over shirt. Glue hair in place. Glue on kerchief. Tie kerchief at the chin.

Nuts and rocks were often used to create heads for pioneer dolls. The dolls were wrapped in cloth and the faces were painted. One story tells of a little boy who occupied long winters playing with fourteen "people" made from smooth river rocks. He noticed that several rocks were missing a few weeks before Christmas. His mother had secretly taken the rocks, painted faces, wrapped them in cloth, and placed them under the tree for Christmas morning.

Pioneer Frills and Necessities

Covered wagons carried items essential for survival and for setting up a home—furniture, food, blankets, tools, glasses, and clocks. Occasionally pioneers had a corner for such sentimental, frivolous items as a bedspread, shawl, set of china dishes, or jewelry. When the pioneers arrived in the Salt Lake Valley and other regions in the West, they had to create most necessities from simple resources. A "make do or do without" philosophy prevailed.

CAN YOU FIND a book with hair samples, a velvet hat, a wedding shoe, a

spur, a lacy veil, a picture of a girl, a wooden washboard, and part of a crazy quilt? *Answers on page 83.*

PUNCH-A-CAN LANTERN

Punch-a-Can Lantern

Materials: any size tin can (a 16-ounce or 29-ounce size works well), water, freezer, nail, hammer, pencil, paper, masking tape, old towel, black spray paint, a short candle, wire for handle (optional).

1. Wash the can and fill it with water. Freeze until the water is solid ice.

2. Draw your idea for a design on paper large enough to wrap around the can. Remove can from freezer and tape your design to the can.

3. Lay the can on a folded towel and punch out the design. Remove paper and tape. Let ice melt enough so that it can be removed from the can.

4. Place your lantern upside down on a protected surface and spray it with black spray paint. Let the paint dry. *Work in a well-ventilated area only!*

5. Place candle in lantern. You may wish to make a wire handle. Light candle and admire your glowing design.

This tin can lantern is useful and fun. Pioneers punched tin lanterns to decorate them. They also punched tin cupboards and chests.

POUNDED PLANT PRINTS

POUNDED PLANT PRINTS

Materials: several sheets of plain, ink-free newsprint (can be obtained for a low fee at most printing companies), just-picked leaves and flowers, hammer, 100%-cotton fabric, washing soda (can be purchased from supermarkets), hard surface for hammering (such as a sidewalk or sturdy table).

1. Gather plants. Choose thin, flat leaves; juicy leaves do not work well. If you want to print flowers, choose small, bright flowers like pansies, violas, and baby carnations. Remember, you never know how the dye is going to transfer to the fabric. The surprise is part of the fun.

2. Cover a hard surface with 8 to 10 newsprint pages. Place a piece of fabric on the newsprint. *We strongly recommend testing several plant parts on scrap pieces of fabric.*

3. Place a leaf or flower on the fabric. Cover the plant with a double layer of newsprint.

4. Hammer the newsprint covering the plant. The tannin coloring in the plant will transfer to the fabric. Carefully lift your paper cover to see if your plant design is getting fully transferred to the cloth.

5. Dip cloth in a solution of washing soda and water. Portions are 1/2 cup washing soda to 2 cups water. The green tannin of the leaves "fixes" successfully with the washing soda solution. After "fixing" the colors, wash your cotton in soapy water, rinse, and dry. All flower petals "fix" differently. Many pinks and purples "fix" aqua and bright blue.

6. After you have experimented with your garden choices and washed and dried your test pieces, you are ready to make a final design on your sampler or other cotton piece.

A sampler was often considered a practice piece for young girls. The piece was designed by the girl and sewn with many colors of thread, allowing her to perfect new stitches. The finished sampler was displayed prominently in the home. Samplers were prized by pioneer thread experts and were passed on to the next generation.

One pioneer child wrote of her sampler days, "Aunt Nancy reeled the silk from some cocoons and dyed skeins which we used for our artwork. These we put in suitable frames, so for years the Lord's Prayer, the Ten Commandments, and 'God Bless Our Home' were ever before us."

Practical as well as decorative, samplers taught children sewing skills that would be applied to lace-making, mending, darning, hemming, and tatting. Children also stitched their ABCs. Many times a family tree was embroidered by weaving hair into the stitches.

Leaves and flowers make handsome samplers. Think of other things you could make. Ivy, shamrock, and rose leaves work quite well. Purple-hued leaves make a nice contrast. Jade plant–type leaves do not work well. Flowers that have bushy blossoms, such as roses, transfer well only if single petals are used.

Rubbings

RUBBINGS

Materials: dark-colored crayons with the paper removed, lightweight paper, tape, surfaces with raised patterns and pictures.

1. Rubbings are traditionally made in graveyards. You can discover some interesting information about early settlers by visiting an old graveyard. You might see a stone on which you can make a rubbing.

2. Peel off the paper from dark-colored crayons. Break them in half.

3. Tape paper to surface of image to be transferred. Rub crayon on the paper or use crayon any way you must to transfer the design.

Try rubbing coins, fossils, dishes, silverware, manhole covers, shells, medals, keys, and other textured surfaces.

Honey Candy

HONEY CANDY

Materials: honey, sugar, cream, heavy saucepan, waxed paper, butter, cookie sheet, any wrapping materials for gift giving.

1. Make the honey candy recipe:

HONEY CANDY
    2 cups honey
    1 cup sugar
    1 cup heavy cream

Combine the ingredients in a heavy saucepan and cook, stirring constantly, about 30 minutes on medium heat. The candy is ready when it reaches the hard-ball stage. To test, drop a bit of the liquid candy into a glass of cold water; it will form a firm ball when ready. Pour the hot candy onto a buttered cookie sheet. Let it cool until you can pull off sections and handle them. Butter your hands and pull the taffylike candy until it is stiff and you can pull it into a ropelike shape.

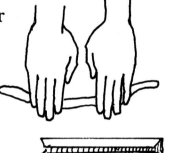

2. Pull into ropes 1 inch wide and let cool on buttered cookie sheet.

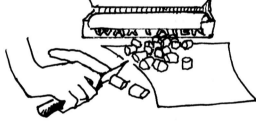

3. Cut ropes into 1-inch to 2-inch slices and wrap in waxed paper.

Of course, the people who chose the beehive as their symbol (the Mormons) had to excel in dishes made from honey. This authentic old recipe for candy was made with honey from a pioneer family's bees and is a traditional favorite even today.

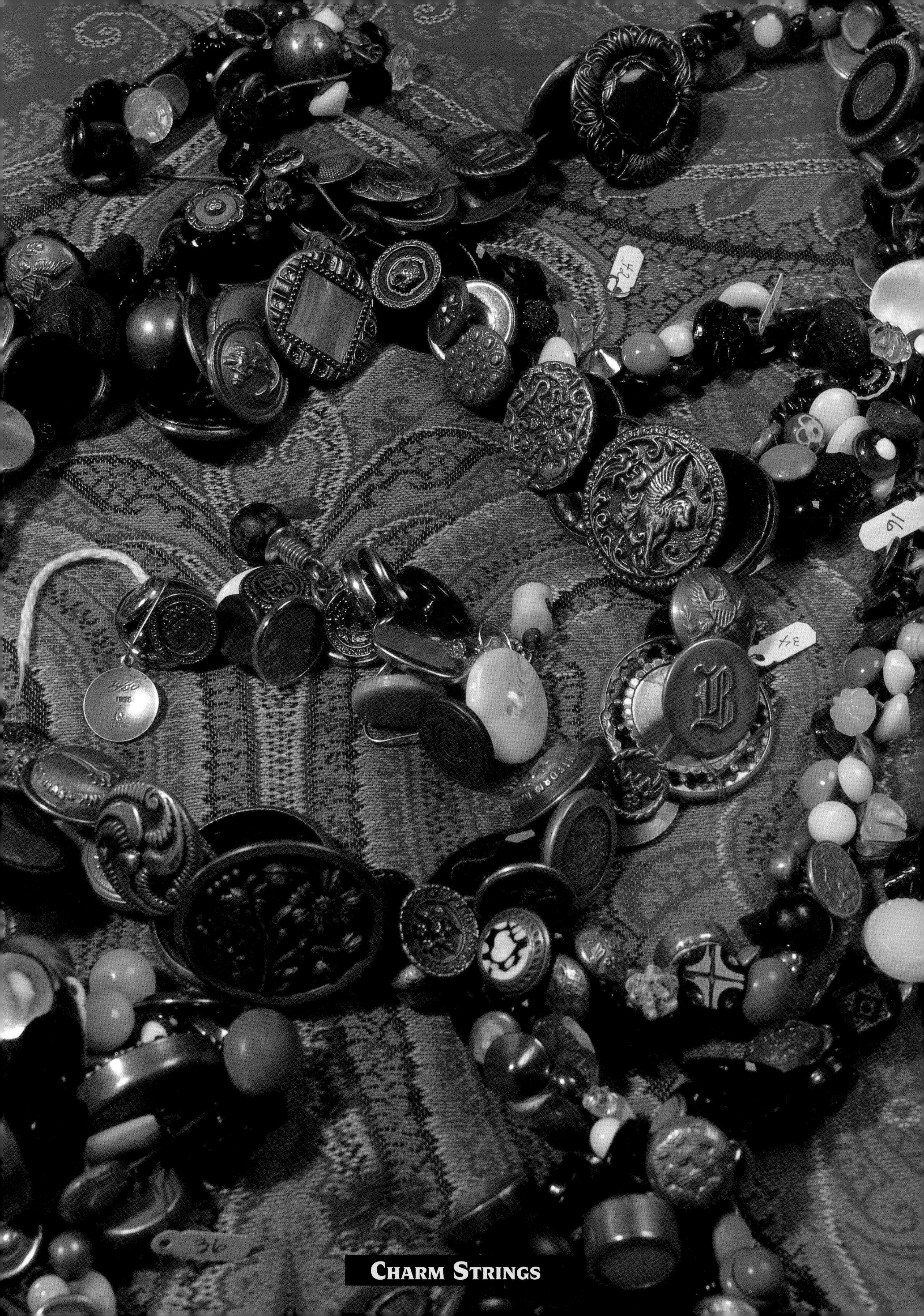

CHARM STRINGS

CHARM STRINGS

Materials: as many pretty buttons as you can gather, elastic string at least 12 inches long, needle, charms, metal badges, and other favorite baubles.

1. Collect unusual objects to make your charm string more interesting and to have it reflect your individuality and creativity.

2. String the first button onto the elastic thread. Tie a knot securely to keep the button in place.

3. String three more buttons and tie a tight knot. The four buttons pulled tightly together make a four-sided, boxlike shape.

4. Continue stringing the buttons in groups of four until your charm string is completed. Collect buttons and make delightful friendship bracelets for your friends.

Despite their limited resources, pioneer girls collected buttons. Prized buttons were strung together to create charm strings. The goal was to collect 999 buttons; the 1,000th was to be presented by a girl's true love.

Charm strings became popular storytelling props because each button had a history. Some strings also included school medals, tiny nut carvings, coins, and charms.

VEGGIE PRINTS

Veggie Prints

Materials: hard vegetables (such as potatoes, carrots, or turnips); small safe knife or sharp pencil; acrylic or tempera paint; sponge, rag, or cheap brush; water; cloth or paper; tray for paint; roller (optional).

1. Choose your vegetable. Potatoes work best. Slice the vegetable lengthwise.

2. Draw a design by digging with a sharp pencil into the vegetable flesh. With the knife, carve away the sides so that the design is about 1/4 inch higher than the edge. Here are some pioneer design ideas: seagull, rose, sego lily, wagon wheel, sunburst, beehive, and temple.

3. Pour paint into a paint tray or foil-covered pan. *If your paint tray is lined with foil, the cleanup is quick and easy.* You may want to smooth out the paint using a roller.

4. Press the image into the paint or brush paint onto the image with a sponge, rag, or brush. Stamp the image on the paper you want to decorate. *Experiment by testing your image on a piece of scrap paper.*

Roll paint.

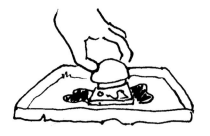
Press image into paint.

Brush paint on image.

5. Let dry and try some of the ideas on the following page.

PRINT WRAPPING PAPER

Custom design your own wrapping paper. Butcher paper works best for prints.

PRINT A FAN

Follow these steps to create a beautiful fan.

1. Fold paper in half. Draw two sides of a triangle, curving one of the sides as shown. Cut out shape.

2. Print designs on the flat fan shape.

3. Mark lines for the fan pleats by using a ruler and scoring with a non-cutting pointed tool, such as the back edge of a butter knife. Mark lines every inch on the curved part of the fan. Pleat accordion-style along the lines.

PRINT A SAMPLER

Use veggie printing to print a border for a quotation or drawing.

PRINT A FLOWER POT

Use *acrylic* paint and a pot made out of unglazed pottery to create a custom-designed flower pot.

Vegetables can be cut, carved, and brushed with paint and then stamped on paper to print wrapping paper and other items. Vegetables are inexpensive, accessible, safe to carve, and easy for little hands to hold.

CAN YOU FIND the beehive made of rope, the woven face of Brigham Young

PIONEER SYMBOLS

As the pioneer population grew in the West, the people developed symbols which were meant to inspire and uplift. The pioneers embedded their values and cultural independence in the symbols that they carved, baked, etched, cast in metal, and embroidered. Beehives represent industry. Clasped hands symbolize loyalty and friendship. The sego lily expresses beauty and survival. The temple is a token of worship and sacred ordinances.

a painted sego lily, flying carved seagulls, the temple, and how many more beehives? *Answers on page 83.*

PIONEER GREETING CARDS

PIONEER GREETING CARDS

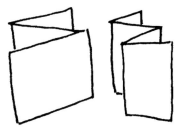

Materials: quality white or colored paper stock or card stock, scissors, crayons or markers, ruler, patterns on pages 66 to 68.

1. Look at the pattern ideas on this page. Choose a pattern from pages 66 to 68.

2. Fold your card or paper stock into thirds or fourths, depending on how many parts are in the pattern you chose. *A ruler might help your accuracy.*

3. On the folded paper, draw or trace the pattern on the front and on the back as needed so that the pattern will show after the paper is cut and folded. *It is a little tricky to do this right.*

4. Carefully cut around shapes and on lines where needed.

5. Color and decorate your layered card.

Pioneers who could afford them gave ornate greeting cards. The cards were beautifully cut and decorated with expressions of love and friendship.

One expression was "May there be just enough clouds in your life to cause a glorious sunset." Others were "As sure as the grass grows round the stump, you are my darling sugar lump" and "As I was sliding on the ice, I thought you were so very nice. I picked you out from all the rest and thought you were the very best."

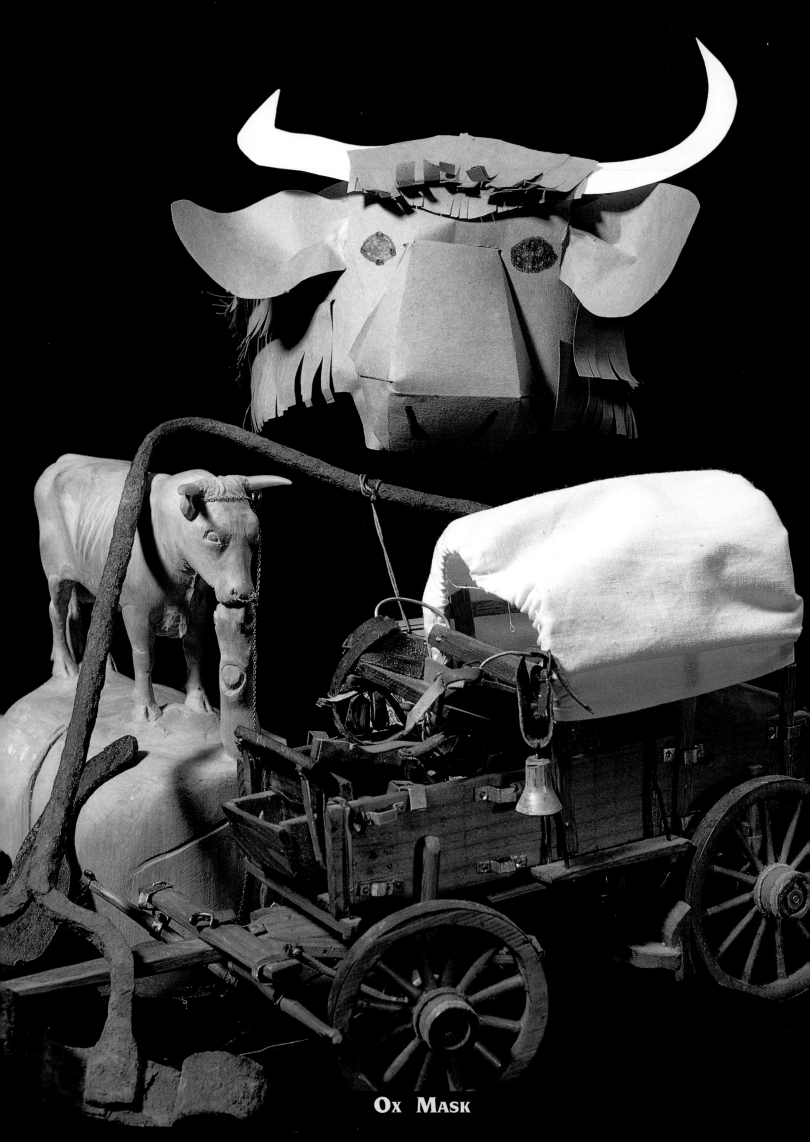

OX MASK

Ox Mask

Materials: brown grocery bag, butcher paper or brown craft paper, file folder cardboard for horns, scissors, black marker, glue, tape, stapler, ruler, patterns on pages 69 to 70.

1. Transfer mask pattern onto brown paper, decreasing or increasing the headband after you have measured the wearer's head.

2. Cut out patterns with scissors. Where pattern indicates, score with scissor point or nail point and a ruler.

3. Glue horns to forehead.

4. Create 3/4-inch fringe pieces for forehead piece and side strips. Oxen were furry but not shaggy; their coats were shorthaired.

5. Glue forehead fringe over center of horns. Glue overlapping strips on sides. Start strips from bottom, gluing or stapling each one at top edge.

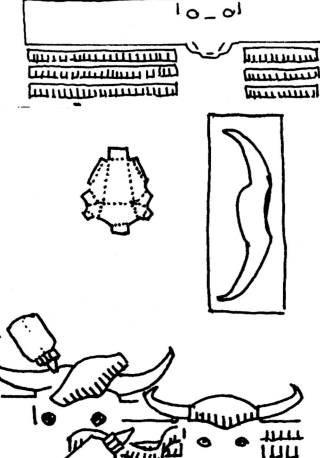

6. To make the ears, fold A over to touch B. Slip folded ends of ears into ear slots and tape down.

7. To make the nose, fold edges under. Fold on scored lines. On each side of nose, fold A over to touch B. Securely glue together areas marked with diagonal lines (////////). Let mask dry. Slip the tabs into slots on forehead piece and tape on the underside. Draw nostrils and eyes with a black or dark brown marker.

8. Adjust headband. Staple or tape securely at back.

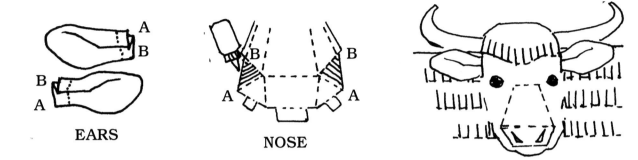

EARS   NOSE

Dress up as oxen and play "crossing the plains." For several reasons, pioneers used oxen rather than horses or mules in their trek west. Oxen were less expensive and easier to train. They adjusted well to hot or cold climates and were less susceptible to disease.

While a horse could pull a load quickly over smooth terrain, oxen could slowly pull a heavier load over rough ground.

Once the pioneers reached the Salt Lake Valley, oxen continued their work—tilling the parched ground for crops, pulling lumber from the canyons for buildings, and hauling huge granite blocks for the Salt Lake Temple from the quarry 20 miles distant.

SEGO LILY CROWN

SEGO LILY CROWN

Materials: yellow poster board or butcher paper; white, yellow, green, and blue scraps of construction paper; scissors; paint or markers; pencil; hole punch; glue; stapler; pattern on page 71.

1. From poster board or butcher paper, cut a headband that is 2 inches by 30 inches. Cut headband to size of head.

2. Trace petals onto white paper and cut out enough for 4 lilies— 4 tops and 8 sides. Color or paint the tips and bases of the petals bluish-purple. Curl tips by rolling them around a pencil.

3. On *blue* construction paper, trace 12 small center petals. Cut out. Color or paint the base areas purple.

4. On *green* construction paper, trace 12 leaves. Cut out. Fold lengthwise.

5. On *yellow* construction paper, use a hole punch to make 8 to 10 tiny circles for each lily.

6. Glue white petals together; the tips of smaller side petals overlap the bottom tip of the larger top petal. Glue on small blue center petals. Glue on yellow circles. Glue leaves to back with bottom center leaf shorter than top leaves.

7. Space lilies around headband. Glue in place. Staple back of headband.

A Ute Indian legend tells of a bloody battle that ended in defeat. When the dead were removed, the battlefield was covered with sego lilies. From that time forward, fields with the flowers were not used in battle. The edible bulb saved the Indians from starvation many times. Pioneers too learned to eat the bulbs when they were hungry. Thistle bulbs were added to a stew, making it taste like potato soup.

Today the sego lily is the Utah state flower. Sego lilies are scarce, and it is illegal to dig them up.

PAPER CHAINS

PAPER CHAINS

Materials: large sheet of brightly colored paper (such as butcher paper, construction paper, wrapping paper, or wallpaper), scissors, pencil, sponge or rag, water-based paint, tray for paint, glue or tape, patterns on pages 71 to 73.

1. Cut the paper into strips 5 to 7 inches wide and as long as possible.

2. Fold the strip accordion-style into 3 or 4 sections. Cut off any excess paper.

3. Choose a pattern from pages 71–73.

4. With your pencil, trace the pattern from our pattern pages or design your own. Make certain that some part of the design extends at least to the folded sides so that when it is cut out the shapes will be connected.

5. If you want to paint the paper with a sponge, do so and let the paint dry. Fold the strip again and cut out the shape you have drawn. To keep the layers of paper from sliding around while you cut, staple or paper clip the layers together on the part of your paper that will be cut away.

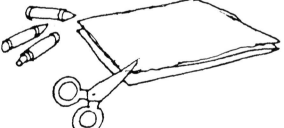

6. Repeat as desired until you have several strips. Fasten together the parts of your paper chain using glue or tape.

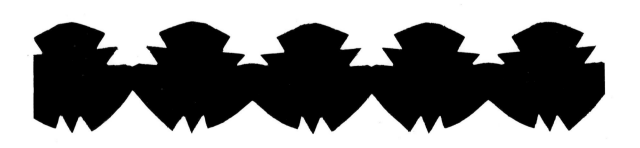

TIPS FOR CUTTING PAPER CHAINS

- Good papers for cutting are origami-printed papers, quality bond paper, decorative gift wrap, wallpaper from sample books, and construction paper.
- Construction paper may be too bulky to cut when folded to more than two thicknesses.
- Paper clips or staples will hold the folds in place while you cut your chains.
- An adult can help you cut small areas with a utility knife.
- Your work may be simplified by *not* cutting small areas such as spaces between the spokes of a wheel or spaces between an ox's legs. You may want to color the small spaces instead.

TIP FOR SPONGE-PAINTING YOUR PAPER CHAINS

- Fill a shallow tray with paint. Touch your sponge onto the surface of the paint-filled tray and *lightly* daub your laid-out paper. Let it dry before folding. Try more than one color of paint.

The first pioneer homes in the Salt Lake Valley were crude adobe and log cabins. The floors were made from packed dirt. Pioneer homemakers tried to beautify their homes by hanging worn cloth on the windows or by adding color wherever possible.

Paper chains of newspaper were carefully cut to form decorative trims, then colored and hung along the edges of rough shelves. Sponge and rag painting were popular with early settlers who lacked brushes. Use paper chains as Christmas tree decorations, as gift cards, or as borders for bulletin boards.

Wind Sock

WIND SOCK

Materials: 24-inch by 36-inch piece of butcher paper (any color), 1-inch by 24-inch cardboard strip, glue, scissors, stapler, paper scraps, crepe paper or ribbons for streamers, art supplies (such as crayons, markers, oil pastels, or water colors), hole punch, 3 1-foot lengths of string, a 10-foot length of string or long pole (optional), patterns on pages 74 and 75.

1. Fold the butcher paper in half lengthwise. Unfold the paper and make a 2-inch fold on one end of the paper as shown. This fold will later hold a strip of cardboard.

2. Return the paper to its folded position, but keep the 2-inch fold on the inside as shown.

3. Choose the wild-rose pattern or the beehive pattern. Trace the pattern onto colored construction paper. Cut out pieces. Decorate them with markers, crayons, or whatever you choose.

4. Glue roses and leaves or beehives and dancing bees onto the wind sock. Let the glue dry.

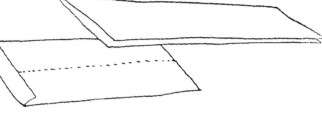

The desert

shall blossom

as a rose

5. Open up your wind sock and glue the 1-inch by 24-inch cardboard strip along the 2-inch fold. With the help of a friend, bend the cardboard strip into a circle and overlap the ends slightly. Fasten the ends of the cardboard strip with several staples. Hold the wind sock in cylinder form and glue the long edges together.

6. Punch 3 equally spaced holes in the cardboard strip. Tie a 1-foot length of string to each hole. Tie or tape the ends of the strings to a long piece of string or a long pole.

7. Make long streamers from the crepe paper or ribbons. With glue or tape, attach to the inside of the tail (the end opposite the cardboard strip).

One of the wind socks shown here is decorated with a rose design. Isaiah foresaw a day that Israel would be gathered and the desert would "blossom as a rose" (Isaiah 35:1). The Mormon pioneers believed this prophecy applied to their labors in settling the West and the symbol inspired their efforts.

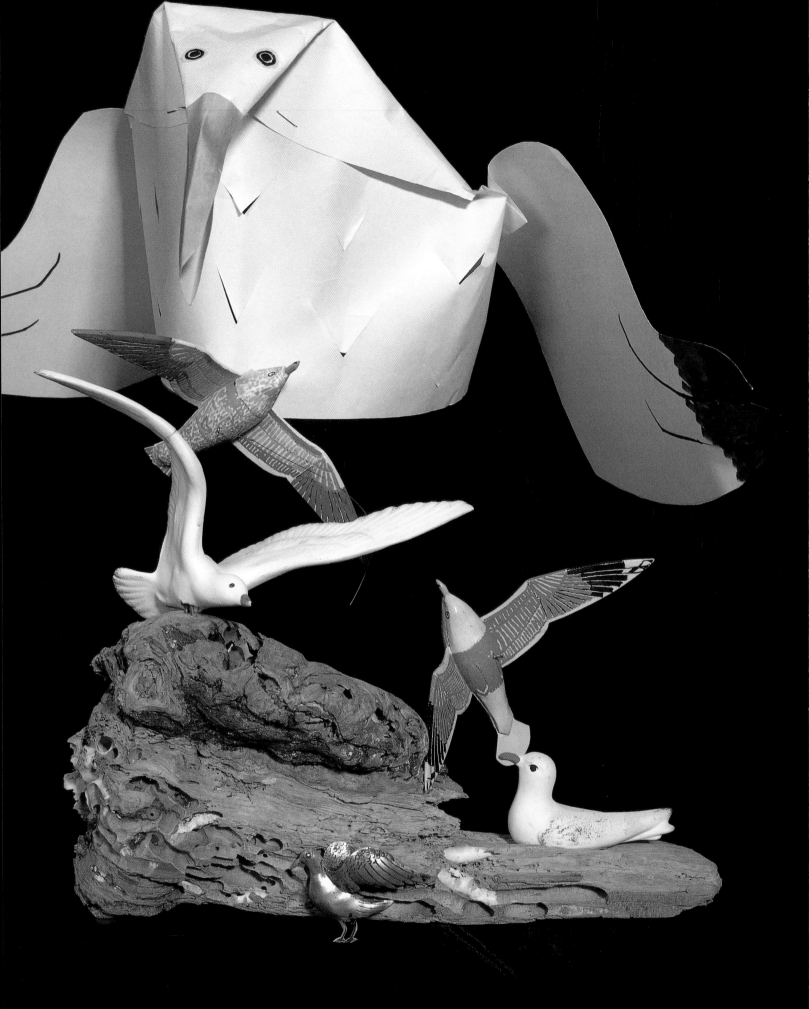

SEAGULL MASK

SEAGULL MASK

Materials: white craft paper or butcher paper, orange construction paper, scissors, yellow and orange markers for eyes and beak, black marker, glue, stapler, pattern on pages 76 and 77.

1. Transfer the mask pattern onto white paper by photocopying it or by drawing it with a marker. If you want to hold the mask on even better, add an additional headband strip. Transfer beak patterns to orange construction paper.

2. Cut out patterns. Score lightly where pattern indicates. Cut 2 1/2-inch diameter eyes. Color eyes with yellow marker.

3. Clip wing feathers and front feather Vs.

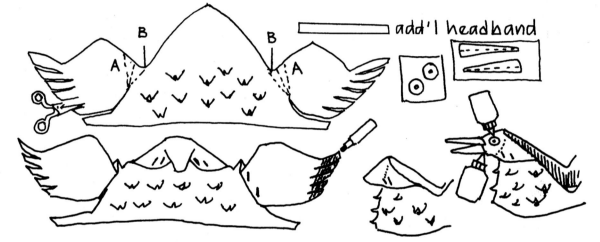

4. Fold wings at A on the dotted lines so that they touch B. Staple folded wings.

5. Fold each side of neck on dotted line C so that edges of neck touch D (see pattern on page 77). Staple folded sides of neck.

6. Glue top and bottom of beak to head. Glue on eyes. With black marker, color wing tips and eye pupils.

7. Adjust headband; staple or tape to appropriate length.

The Great Salt Lake, to the west of Salt Lake City, is home to a wide variety of gulls. The Utah state bird is the California Seagull, the bird pictured most often in pioneer stories.

BREAD-DOUGH BEEHIVE AND BEES

BREAD-DOUGH BEEHIVE AND BEES

Materials: ingredients for bread dough (or buy frozen bread dough), cookie sheet, spatula, surface for kneading dough and rolling strips, large mixing bowl, beaten egg yolk, chocolate frosting in applicator tube (or buy ready-made frosting in an applicator tube), brown pipe cleaners, toothpicks, pattern on page 78.

BEEHIVE

1. Make bread dough.

RECIPE FOR BREAD DOUGH

(Makes 2 15-inch beehives and 4 to 8 bees)

      1 tablespoon yeast
      3 tablespoons sugar or honey
      2 cups warm water
      2 teaspoons salt
      1/4 cup oil
      7 cups flour

Mix sugar or honey in warm (not hot) water. Add yeast and let stand for 5 minutes to get yeast working. Add salt and oil. Add flour a little at a time until you can work the dough with your hands. Add more flour if the dough is sticky. Knead.

2. Cut out the beehive pattern on page 78. Grease a cookie sheet. In the grease, trace the outline of the pattern with your finger. *You may make your beehive any size you wish. Our pattern fills a standard cookie sheet.*

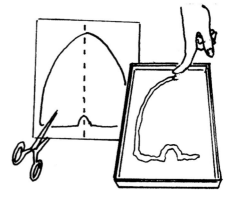

3. Put aside about 1 cup of dough for the bees. Divide the remaining dough into an even number of equal-sized balls (about 8). Roll balls into long, thin strips.

4. Starting at the top, lay strips one after another (see illustration on page 60). For it to look like a real beehive, make sure your dough strips are the same thickness. After all the strips are placed, cut the edges off to fit the beehive shape.

5. Cut out an entry hole at the bottom of the hive. If you plan to hang your beehive, put a small hole in the middle of the second strip from the top.

6. Let rise for 20 minutes. While the beehive dough is rising, the oven can be preheated and bees may be made. Bake beehive for 30 to 40 minutes at 300 degrees Fahrenheit. Occasionally open your oven door and check on the baking.

7. Remove beehive from oven. Brush your beehive with a beaten egg yolk while it is still hot.

BEES
1. For each bee, roll 1 round and 1 oval shape from the dough. Join them on the greased baking sheet so they will bake joined together.

2. Bake with the beehive but for a much shorter time, 7 minutes or so. Bees may be added to the cookie sheet near the end of the baking.

3. Remove bees from the cookie sheet and cool.

4. With chocolate frosting, put stripes on the back part of the bee's body. Put eyes on the head.

5. Add brown pipe cleaners for antennae and wings. Push a toothpick into the underside of the bee. Insert the other end into the baked and cooled beehive.

Put on stripes and eyes.   Put on antennae and wings.   Insert toothpick.

The beehive represents cohesiveness, productivity, and division of labor. The pioneers aspired to a self-sufficient economy. "Produce what you consume" was Brigham Young's edict. In response, the pioneers built irrigation systems, gristmills, sawmills, ironworks, tanneries, and stockyards. The cooperation, efficiency, and discipline required were tremendous and truly resembled a buzzing hive. Brigham Young's home was called the Beehive House. Carved beehives adorned the roof, stairways, and furniture. The bread-dough beehive is edible and may be served or preserved.

Seagull and Cricket Mobile

SEAGULL AND CRICKET MOBILE

Materials: black and white poster board, 1/8-inch diameter dowel divided into a 20-inch piece and 2 8-inch pieces, scissors, rubber cement or glue, markers or paint, fishing line, yellow paper, pattern on page 79.

1. Trace the seagull pattern onto white poster board. To trace wings, place pattern on poster board, trace, then flip pattern piece at center, mirroring the first half. Make 3 gulls. Cut them out. Decorate the gulls with black marker or paint.

2. Cut slots or score for folding where indicated. Attach gull wings, tail, and feet to the body.

3. Trace the cricket pattern onto black poster board. Be sure to flip pattern so it looks like the illustration below. Make 5 crickets. Cut them out.

4. Crease for folding where indicated. Remove one of the small center legs. The other legs will be folded under the body and glued to the side as a brace.

5. Fold up hind legs and tail pieces.

6. Fold small legs out from body and down. Dab a small amount of rubber cement (works better than glue) or glue near the folds of the hind legs to keep them close to the body.

7. String gulls and crickets with fishing line. Notch the dowel as shown. Attach the gulls to the long dowel and the crickets to the small dowels or to the gulls as shown. Adjust the strings so your mobile will balance.

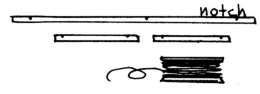

A lovely visual aid, this hanging is a reminder of a famous story, the miracle of the seagulls and the crickets.

The pioneers arrived in the Great Salt Lake Valley during the summer of 1847. The 1848 harvest was vital to their survival. Healthy green sprouts covered 2,000 acres of tilled soil where sagebrush had grown months before. The crop was promising. Then one morning a black mass swarmed from the foothills. Thousands of newly hatched black crickets descended upon the crops. Barren, crop-stripped land lay in their wake.

Families burned, beat, and drowned the bugs for three days and nights, making little difference. The pioneers prayed fervently for help. Suddenly on the fourth day, shrill cries could be heard from the west. Great flocks of seagulls were flying overhead. The seagulls ate the insects and saved the crops! Generations have retold the miracle of the gulls, and the story is confirmed by diaries and newspaper accounts of witnesses.

One of the few monuments in the nation dedicated to a bird is in Salt Lake City. The Seagull Monument reads: "In grateful remembrance of the mercy of God to the Mormon Pioneers."

PATTERN PAGES

Gingerbread Doll Puppets Pattern

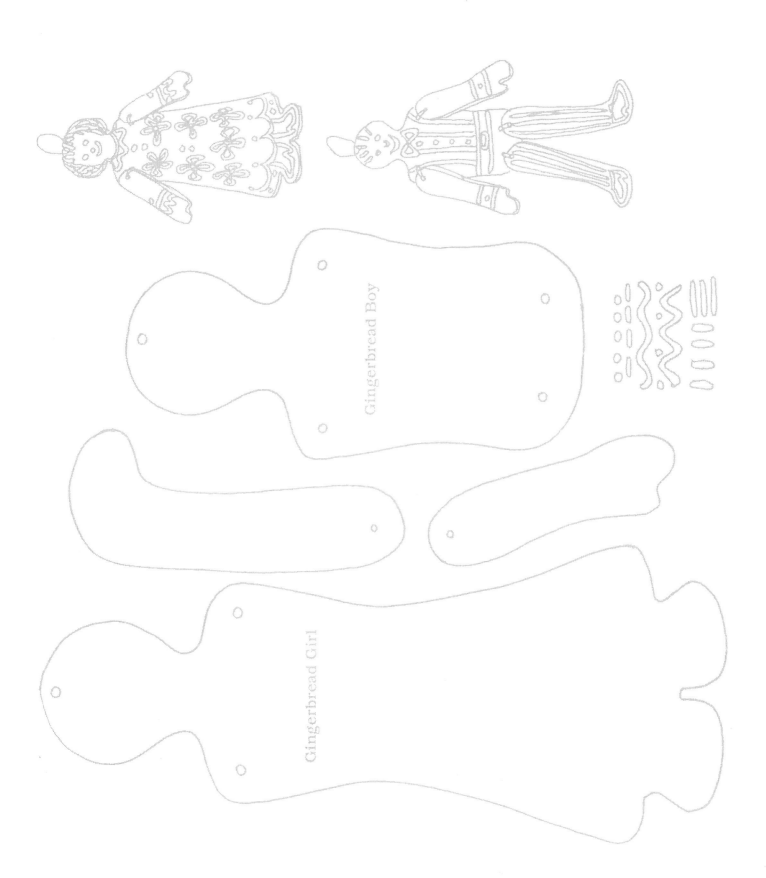

Gingerbread Boy

Gingerbread Girl

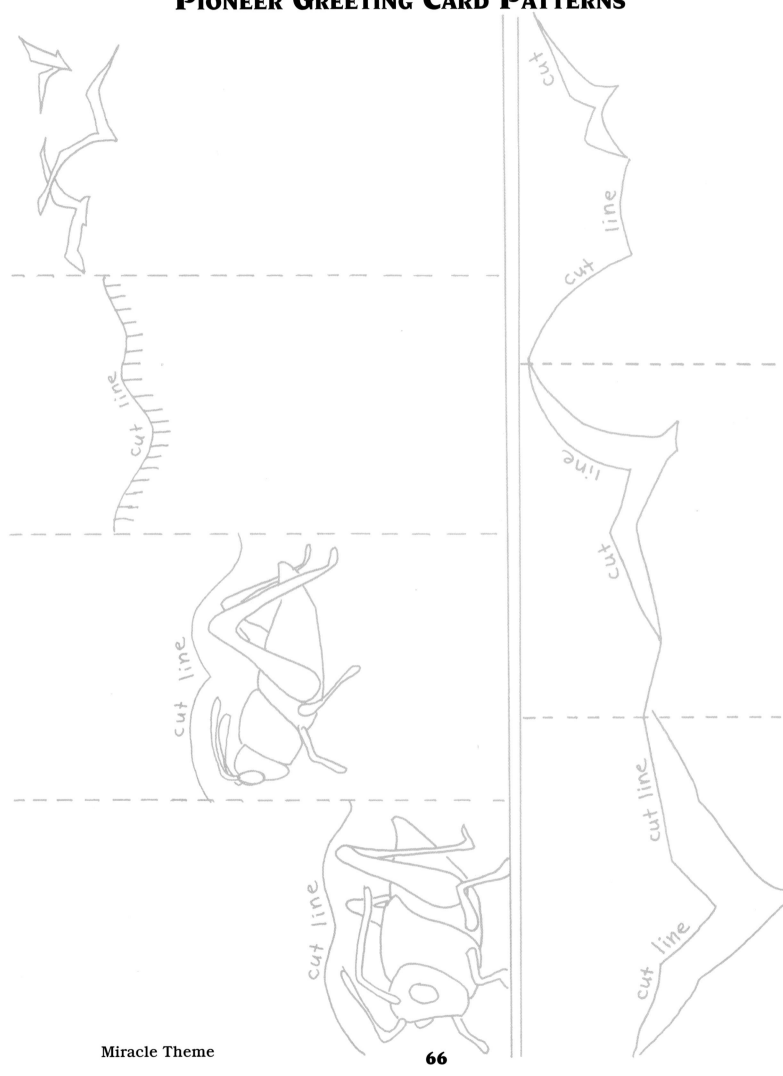

FOLDED GREETING CARD PATTERNS

Beehive Theme

67

Temple Theme

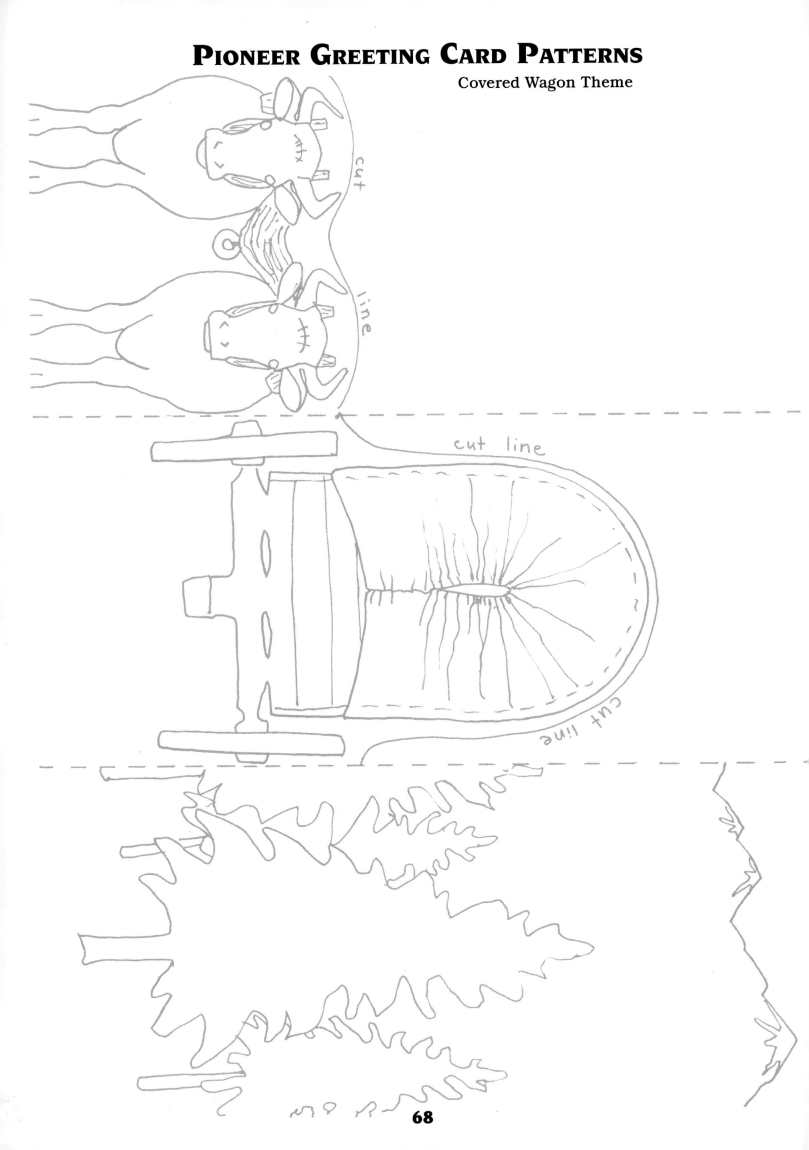

Ox Mask Pattern

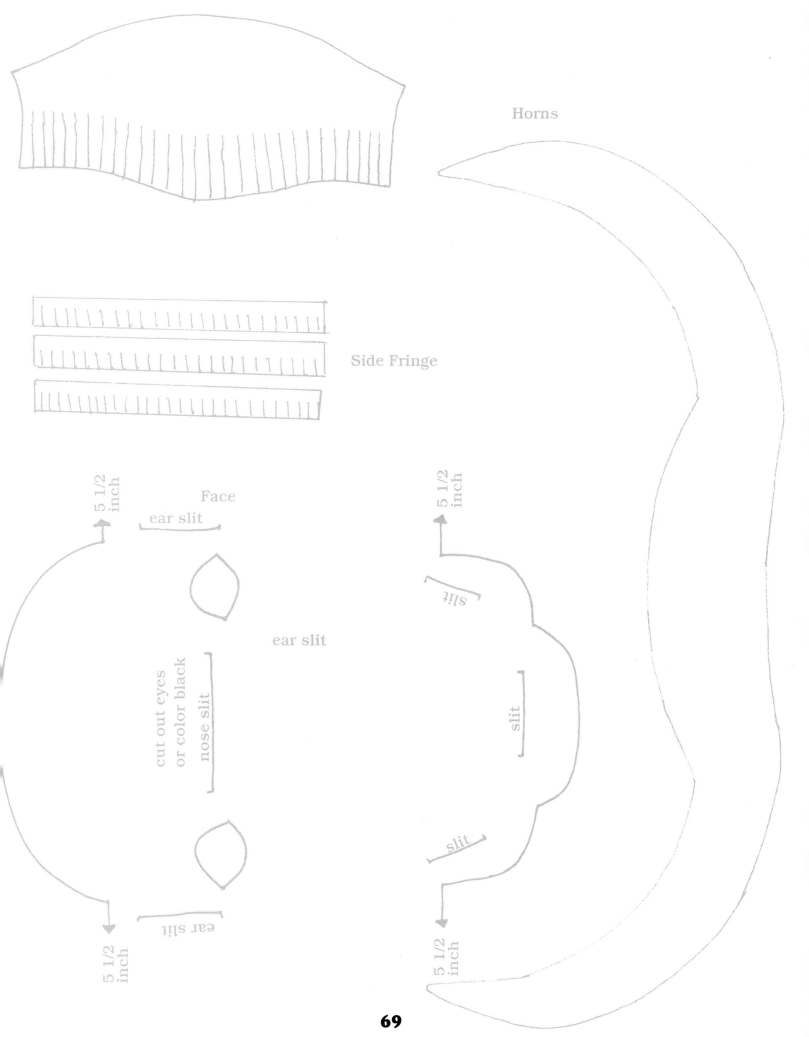

Forehead Fringe

Horns

Side Fringe

5 1/2 inch

Face

ear slit

5 1/2 inch

slit

ear slit

cut out eyes
or color black

nose slit

slit

slit

ear slit

5 1/2 inch

slit

5 1/2 inch

Ox Mask Pattern

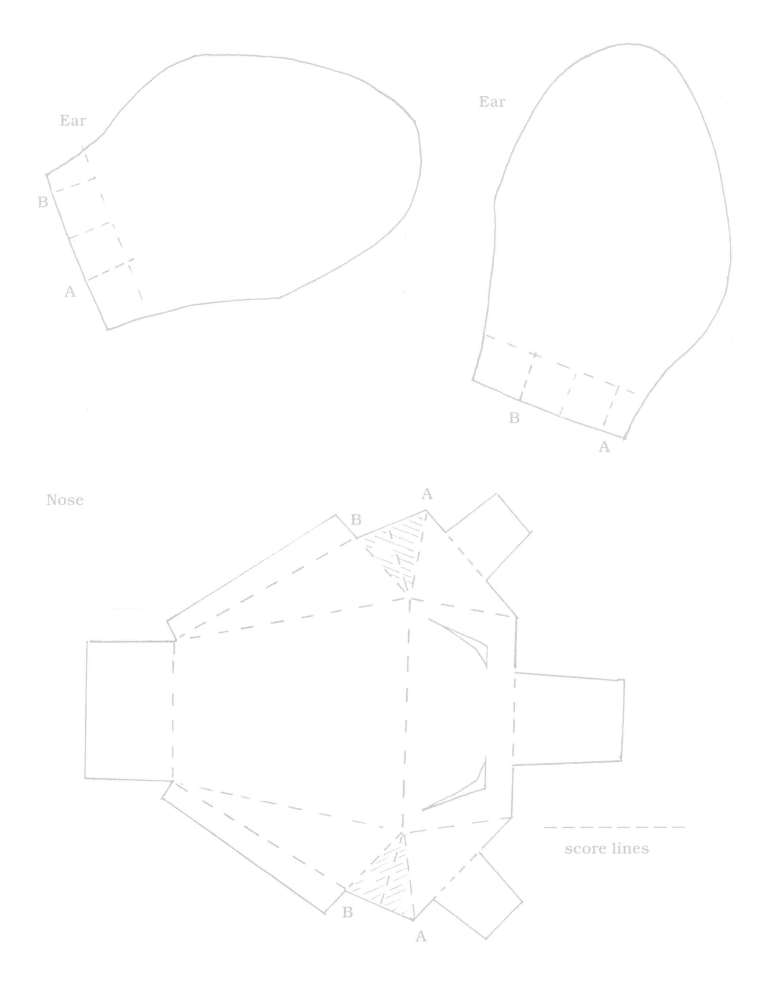

Ear

Ear

B

A

B

A

Nose

A

B

score lines

B

A

Sego Lily Crown Pattern

Paper Chain Patterns

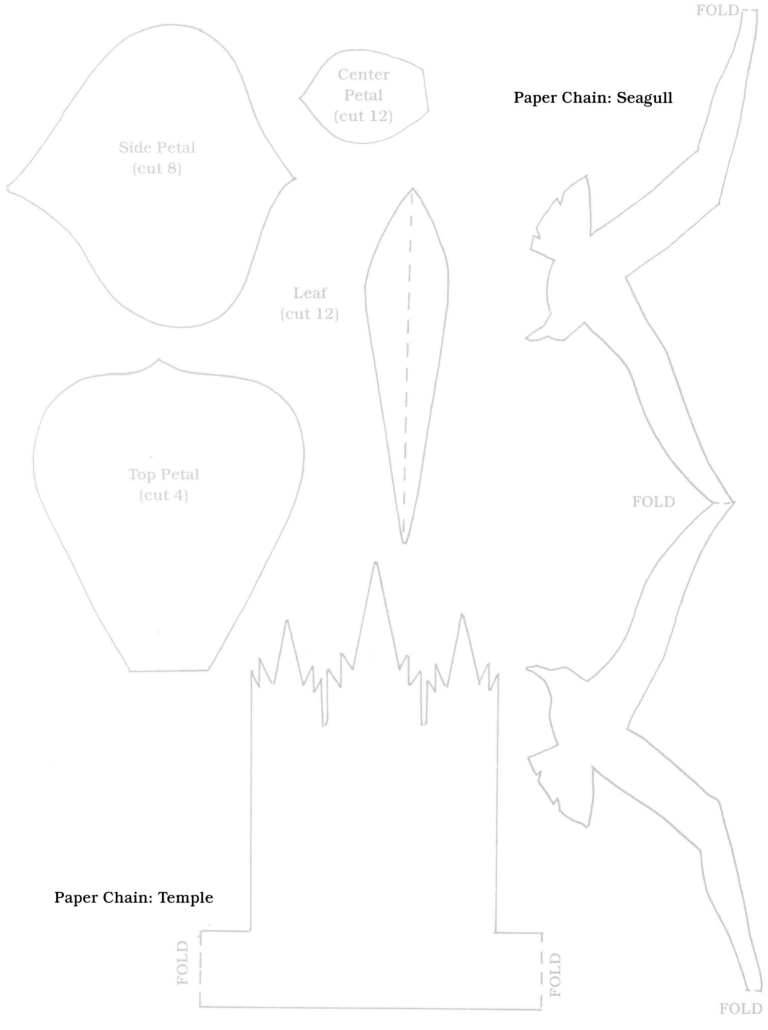

Side Petal
(cut 8)

Center
Petal
(cut 12)

Paper Chain: Seagull

Leaf
(cut 12)

Top Petal
(cut 4)

FOLD

Paper Chain: Temple

FOLD

FOLD

FOLD

FOLD

FOLD

PAPER CHAIN PATTERNS

Paper Chain: Crickets

Paper Chain: Oxen

Paper Chain: Handcart

FOLD

FOLD

FOLD

FOLD

FOLD

FOLD

FOLD

FOLD

PAPER CHAIN PATTERNS

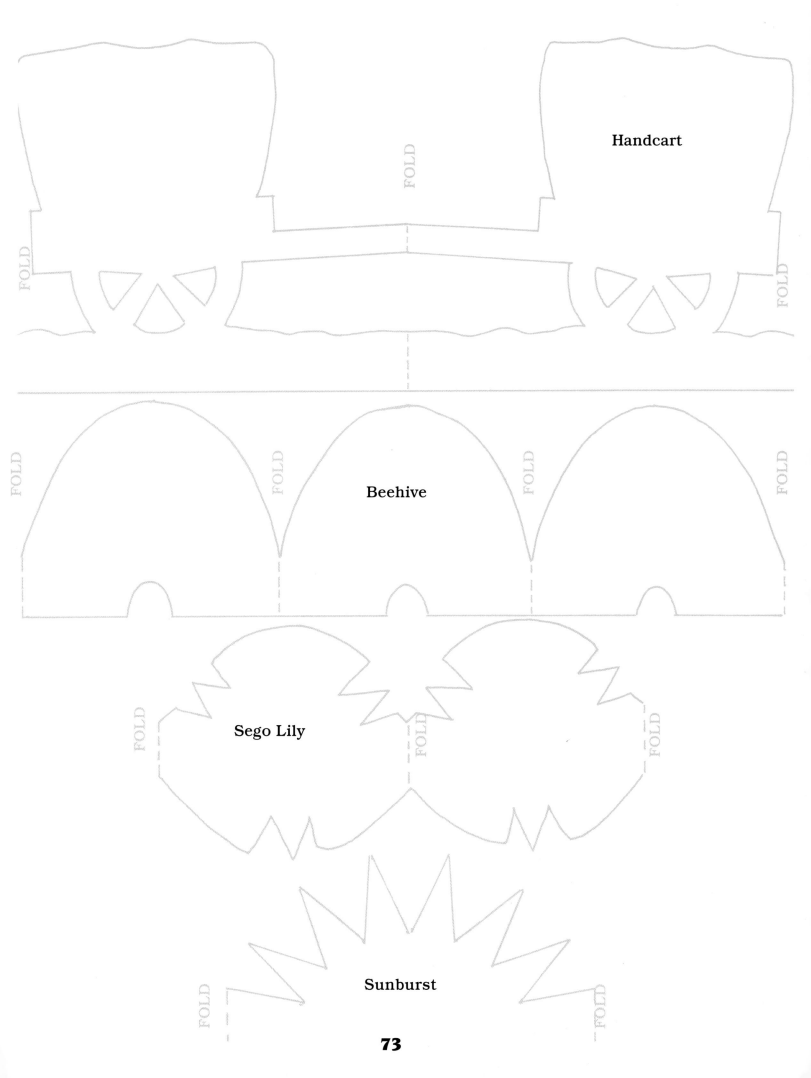

Handcart

Beehive

Sego Lily

Sunburst

ROSE WIND SOCK PATTERN

Beehive Wind Sock Pattern

SEAGULL MASK PATTERN

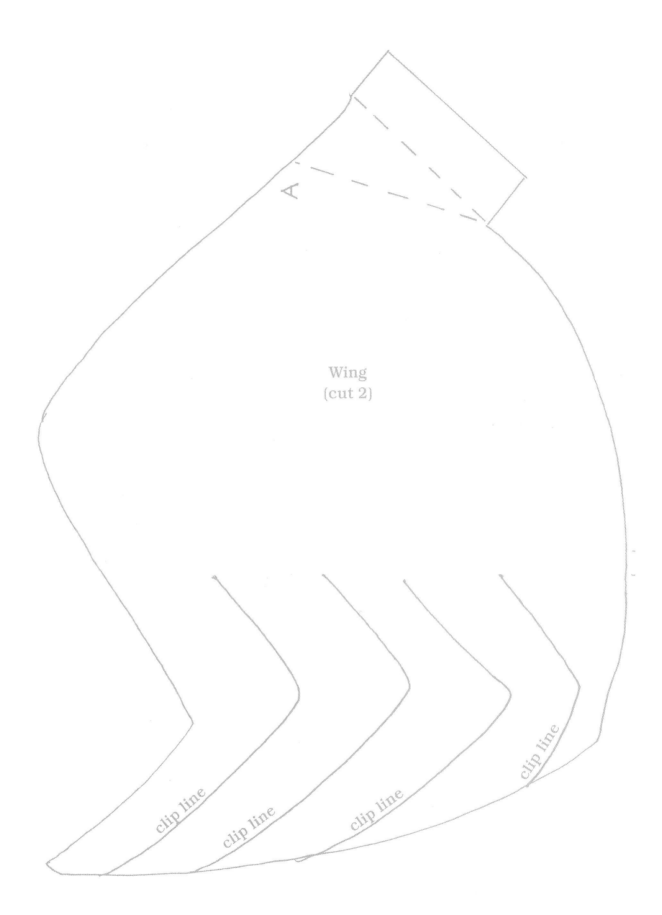

Wing
(cut 2)

clip line

clip line

clip line

clip line

Seagull Mask Pattern

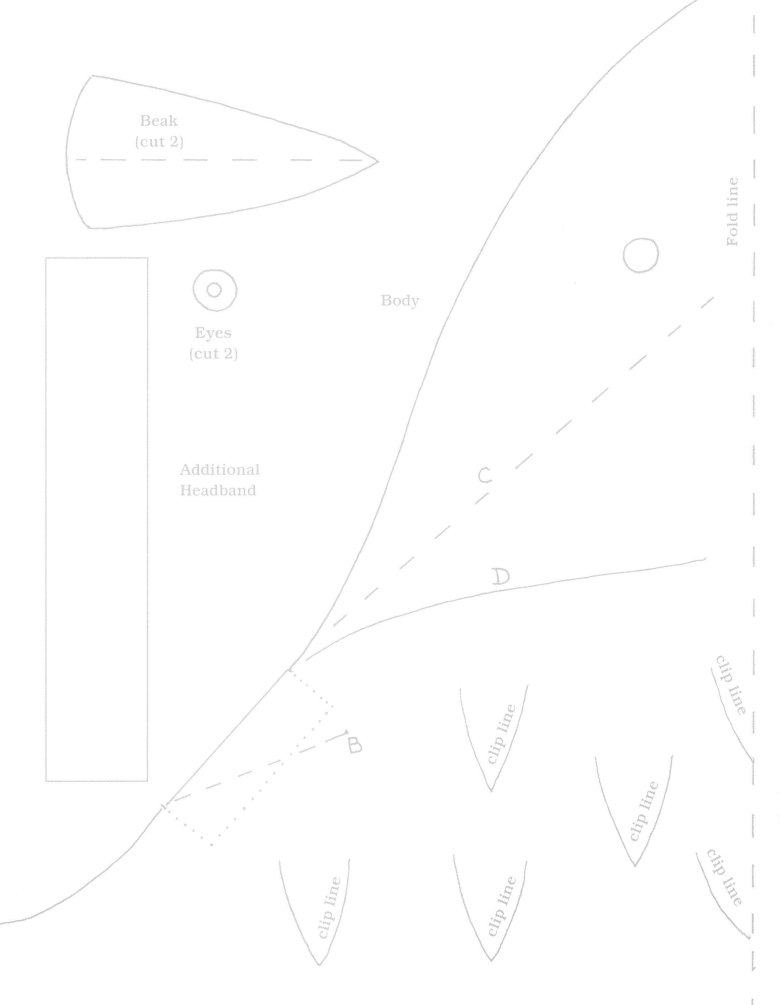

Beak
(cut 2)

Eyes
(cut 2)

Additional
Headband

Body

Fold line

C

D

B

clip line

clip line

clip line

clip line

clip line

clip line

BREAD-DOUGH BEEHIVE AND BEE PATTERN

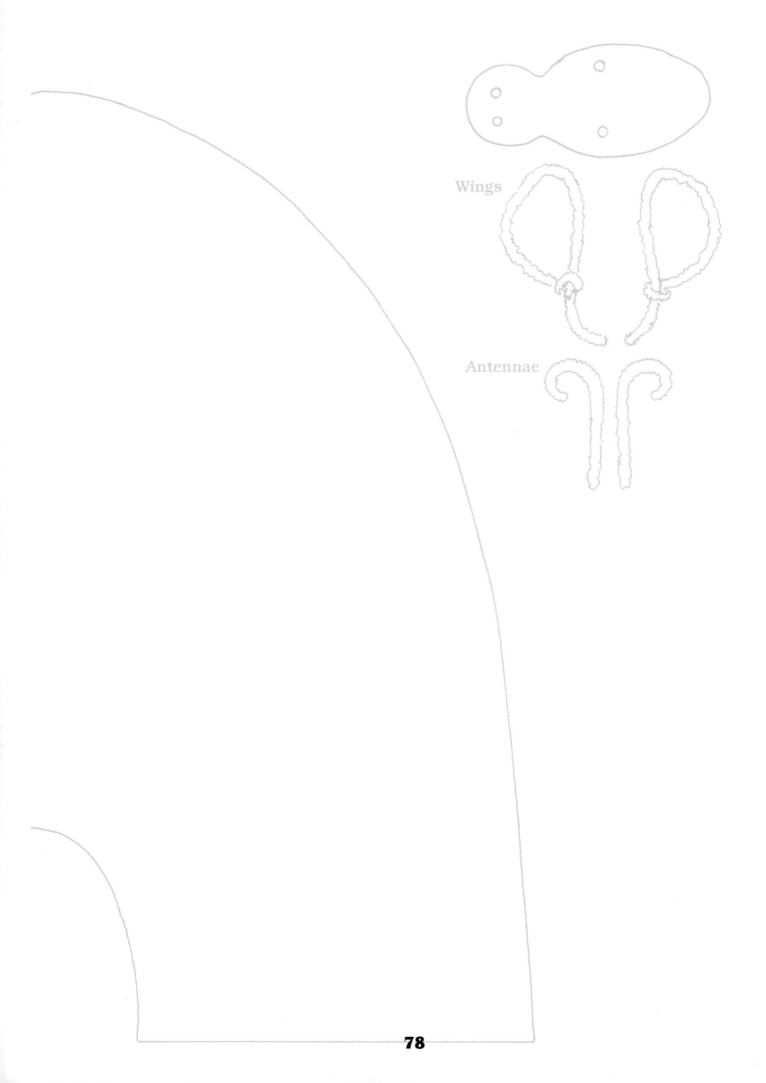

Wings

Antennae

Seagull and Cricket Mobile Pattern

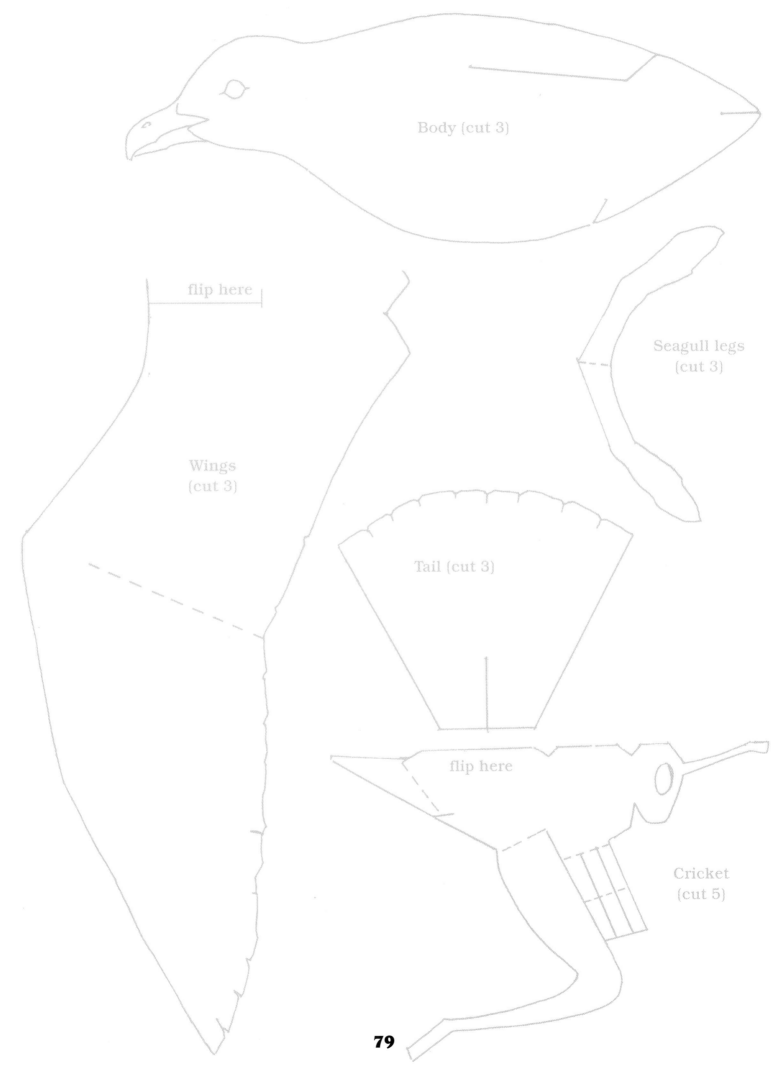

Body (cut 3)

flip here

Seagull legs
(cut 3)

Wings
(cut 3)

Tail (cut 3)

flip here

Cricket
(cut 5)

INDEX

ACKNOWLEDGMENTS

We express special appreciation to the International Society of the Daughters of Utah Pioneers **Pioneer Memorial Museum** in Salt Lake City. Edith Menna, museum director, generously shared the collection with us. We especially thank LaRue Pitts, research specialist, for the volunteer help that she gave in assembling items for our use.

Jack Vigo, artist, painted "Miracle of the Gulls," part of the Pioneer Memorial Museum collection.

Su Richards, volunteer coordinator at Wheeler Historic Farm, contributed valuable research information.

Madlyn Tanner assisted in editing the text.

Dale Beecher, registrar at the Museum of Church History and Art for The Church of Jesus Christ of Latter-day Saints, assisted us in viewing the museum collection and helped with the accuracy of our information. We are especially grateful to the museum director, Dr. Glen Leonard, whose early efforts to germinate the project and whose enthusiasm encouraged us to go forward.

Wilma Young loaned us her handcart and silk sego lily arrangement.

We are grateful to our family members who previewed, tested, and supported our content choices: Wilma Young, Rebecca Richards, Martha Mortensen, Tessa Reinemer, Melinda Tietjen, and Alice Ann Swaner. The combined 16 children all helped considerably.

REFERENCE BOOKS

Allison, Linda. *The Sierra Club Summer Book.* San Francisco: Sierra Club Books, 1977.
Daughters of Utah Pioneers. *An Enduring Legacy: Pioneer and Old Dolls.*
———. *The Pioneer Cook Book.*
———. *Pioneer Memorial Museum: A Collection of Pioneer Memorabilia and Excerpts from Pioneer Journals.* Salt Lake City: National Society of Daughters of Utah Pioneers, 1983.
———. *Pioneer Tales to Tell.* Salt Lake City: Paragon Press, 1989.
Hamilton, Leslie. *Child's Play: 200 Instant Crafts and Activities for Preschoolers.* New York: Crown Publishers, 1989.
Klinkenborg, Verlyn. "Come booooooosss! Come boooossss!" *The Smithsonian Magazine* 24 (September 1993), pp. 81–91.
Paxman, Shirley. *Homespun.* Salt Lake City: Deseret Book Company, 1976.
Time-Life Books. *The Old West: The Pioneers.* Time-Life Publishers, 1974.
Wiseman, Ann. *Making Things: The Handbook of Creative Discovery.* Boston: Little Brown and Company, 1973.

Resource Materials
pages 2 to 3

Pioneer Dolls
pages 18 to 19

1. **Dried weeds** from southern Utah used to make "Brigham Tea."
2. Pot of imported **red dye** called cochineal.
3. **Picked cotton** brought across the plains.
4. **Cotton pod** brought from Kentucky. Cotton was grown in "Dixie," nickname for an area in southern Utah. Brigham Young called 300 families to develop a cotton industry. The soil was alkaline and infested with crickets. Eventually the experiment failed.
5. **Hinged sewing kit**.
6. **Scissors** brought to Utah in 1849.
7. 100-year-old **ribbon and floss**.
8. **Hand-smithed nails**.
9. **Pattern paper** for woman's dress.
10. **Carded flax** ready for spinning.
11. **Sheep shears**.
12. **Marbles** made from clay, some crudely colored with pigment.
13. **Thimble** given as a courtship gift.

14. **Toadstools** gathered and cooked for black dye.
15. **Carding paddles** for cotton, wool, and flax.
16. **Silk cocoons** made by silk worms which were imported and raised for the silk unraveled from the cocoons. Every family was expected to have a mulberry bush in their yard to feed the silk worms.
17. **Handmade lace**.
18. **Flax woven pants** made by Sarah Hurdie in 1840, when she was 12 years old. She grew, carded, and wove the flax herself.
19. **Raw wool**.
20. **Pine cones** for stuffing and dye making
21. **Pine needles** for stuffing dolls and toys
22. **Rag ball** for weaving a rug.
23. **Lace bobbins** for crafting lace.

1. **Twig dolls** crafted especially for this book but adapted from known stick dolls.
2. A **wooden doll** jointed with leather, believed to have been made in 1778. This doll was found in one of Brigham Young's homes.
3. **Pink-cheeked doll** with rag body, brought to Nauvoo, Illinois, in 1844.
4. See no. 1.
5. **Indian baby doll**.
6. **Typical doll** given after arrival in Salt Lake Valley. This doll was bought in 1861.
7. **Hankie doll** crafted for this book, adapted from dolls described by pioneers.
8. **Six-inch doll** bought in 1838 in New York and brought to Nauvoo.
9. **Minerva**, probably bought in 1840s, judging by the clothing style. This doll was first owned by the Thorndell family in Uniontown, Pennsylvania, and has been displayed by 4 generations.

Because the doll was described as "too precious for play," it has always been displayed and is in fine condition.
10. This **150-year-old doll** has leather arms that have been chewed by the children who played with it.
11. It was common for **handmade dolls** to resemble outstanding teachers. This doll represents Mary Jane Dilworth.
12. The **tallest doll** in this photo was handmade in 1865 by the grandmother of Elizabeth H. Whitehead for her while she was away at school. It is called "Welsh design" and has a wooden body and jointed limbs.
13. A **clothespin doll**.
14. **Corn husk doll**.
15. The **oldest doll** in the group picture. This 4-inch doll with real hair is over 200 years old.
16. See no. 14.
17. A **rag doll** with sheep's-wool hair.
18. **Jointed wooden doll** from England called a "ha'penny" doll.

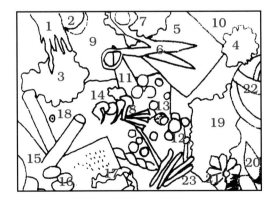

Resource Materials

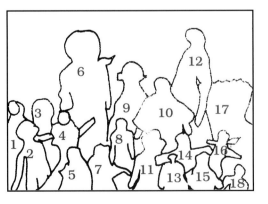

Pioneer Dolls

1. A **watercolor portrait** done in 1848 by an unknown artist in Birmingham, England, brought to the Salt Lake Valley.
2. **Wooden sock form** for blocking handmade socks.
3. **Knit doll tights**.
4. **Crocheted ball**.
5. **Handmade patchwork dress** sewn with thread carefully saved from undoing wagon covers.
6. **Miniature spinning wheel**.
7. **Miniature rocking chair**.
8. **White leather baby shoes**.
9. Never-been-worn **child's shoe** from a co-op store in northern Utah.
10. **Game board**.
11. **Child's black shoe**.
12. **Christening dress** of heavy embroidery.
13. 140-year-old **school photo**.
14. Miniature **doll trunk**.
15. Green painted **tin bucket**.
16. **Straw hat** made from straw grown for weaving.
17. **School slate pencil**.

Pioneer Children's Treasures
pages 6 to 7

1. A lace **veil** worn by pioneer women's leader Emmeline B. Wells.
2. Hubbard **washboard** brought across the plains by Phoebe and Elizabeth Richards.
3. **Autograph book**.
4. **Photo** of Isabelle Price at age fourteen in Birmingham, England, just before she journeyed to Salt Lake. She is wearing a dress she made herself.
5. **Hammer**.
6. **Crazy quilt** made from family clothing by Isabelle Price.
7. **A velvet bonnet**.
8. **Hair sampler book** made in 1845 in Nauvoo, Illinois.
9. **Rose-printed neckpiece**.
10. **Compass** that Truman Angell, architect for the Salt Lake Temple, used in his work.
11. **Woven hair flower wreath** made by Permelia Bassett in 1874.
12. **Spur**.
13. **Wedding shoe**.
14. **Charm bracelet** made as Jubilee Celebration souvenir of 1897.
15. **Basket** made of cloves and beads by prisoner in Sing Sing.

Pioneer Frills and Necessities
pages 24 to 25

1. **Woven wool coverlet** from early Utah Woolen Mills.
2. Hexagon pattern **patchwork quilt**.
3. **Woven banner** for Jubilee Celebration of 1897.
4. Jubilee Celebration **commemorative cup**.
5. Hand-painted sego lily **china cup and plate**.
6. Salt Lake Temple **replica plate**.
7. **Beehive-embroidered tablecloth** made for Rose Ellen Bywater Valentine by 13-year-olds in the German/Austrian mission.
8. **Various souvenirs** from the Jubilee Celebration: beehive salt and pepper shakers, wooden beehives, ceramic beehive honey pot, seagull and beehive pins, cricket paperweight, and ceramic seagulls.
9. **Beehive** made of straw bundled to make a rope.
10. **Carved wooden seagulls**.

Pioneer Symbols
pages 40 to 41

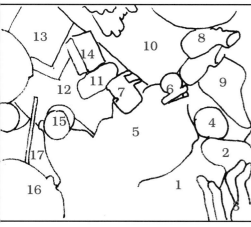

Pioneer Children's Treasures

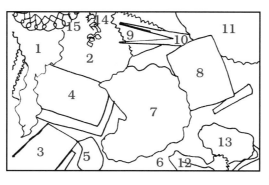

Pioneer Frills and Necessities

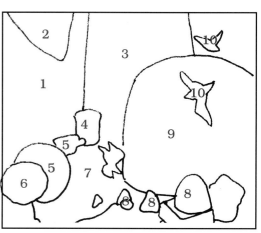

Pioneer Symbols